This book belongs to _____ ,

whose star sign is _____ .

If found, please _____

_____ .

To all the curious minds, sensitive souls, and magical dreamers.

Your inner light will always illuminate the path ahead.

—AK

an imprint of Little Bee Books, Inc.

251 Park Avenue South, New York, NY 10010 | Copyright © 2019 by Aliza Kelly | Illustrations by
Natalya Balnova | Author Photograph by Sofia Szamosi | Additional Image Credits: p. 12 Lascaux
cave (Prof saxx, filter added), p. 13 Roman Coin (courtesy of the British Museum, filter added), Claudius
Ptolemy (Wikipedia Commons, filter added), p. 14 Abu Ma'shar (by Hermann tom Ring, © Bayerische
Staatsgemäldesammlungen, filter added), William Lilly (Wikipedia Commons, filter added), p. 15
Newtonian Telescope Replica (© Andrew Dunn, filter added), p. 17 The White House (Wikipedia
Commons, filter added) | All rights reserved, including the right of reproduction in whole or in part in
any form. | BuzzPop is a trademark of Little Bee Books, Inc., and associated colophon is a trademark of
Little Bee Books, Inc. | Manufactured in the United States of America RRD 0519 | First Edition

1 3 5 7 9 10 8 6 4 2

ISBN 978-1-4998-0967-1

buzzpopbooks.com

Starring You

by
Aliza
Kelly

Table of Contents

Welcome, Cosmic Warrior!

My name is Aliza (pronounced "uh-LEE-zuh") Kelly. I'm a professional astrologer. I spend my days learning about space, history, mythology, and the mysteries of the universe. Every day, I look at the positions of the stars and planets. Then I use both ancient and modern wisdom to discover what cosmic forces are at work upon us. Looking at the world through this lens helps people understand their moods, relationships, and life events. In a sense, I help people get to know themselves.

I first learned about astrology when I was ten years old. It opened up a whole new world for me. It taught me to be kind to myself, and to do my best to understand others. It taught me to love my whole self, including the areas I had thought were flaws. It also taught me that there was no end to what I could learn about my inner world, the universe, and humanity. I want you to have that experience, too.

In this guide, I cover the basics of astrology and how to use it in your daily life. I explain the vocabulary astrologers use, provide cosmic interpretations, and give background on the practice. In the end, you should feel at home in the cosmos.

The ultimate goal is self-knowledge. Through reflection activities, we will uncover your secret desires, hidden talents, and essential truths. Together we'll create a cosmic self-portrait. As you learn more about yourself, your relationships with friends, family, and even (*ahem!*) crushes will improve. It's your universe, so use this guide to shine brightly within it!

I hope these first astrological discoveries will jump-start a lifelong study of the cosmos. At the very least, I hope you'll treasure this snapshot of the beautiful inner you.

All you need to get started is a sense of wonder and your date of birth. You don't need to be psychic or believe in anything specific to use astrology—it's simply about stargazing!

I can't wait to go into the stars with you!

xoxo,

What Is Astrology?

Maybe you're wondering "what is astrology, anyway?" This is a great question, Cosmic Warrior!

Simply put, astrology is cosmic storytelling. Specifically, astrology is the interpretation of the planets, stars, and other celestial bodies in the sky, focusing on how their positions affect us. It may seem a bit complicated at first, but don't worry, you'll catch on quickly!

Here's the deal: The movements of the cosmos are scientifically calculated. Their interpretation, however, is mystical. Astrologers use stories and wisdom passed down through generations to describe how the positions of the celestial bodies affect life on earth.

There are many different types of astrology practiced all over the world. They date back to the Babylonians, who developed the foundations of the tradition. You could argue, though, that astrology started with the dawn of time, when people first looked up at the stars. In many ways, stargazing defines what it means to be human.

I practice Western astrology. It draws on the cultures of ancient Greece and ancient Rome, also known as "classical antiquity."

The ancient Greeks created stories about their many gods and goddesses. In their time, the stories were used to explain forces on earth, like human emotions, weather, life, and death. Today, we call these stories "mythology." Astrologers use mythology to derive meaning from the planets. In fact, we use the names of the ancient gods and goddesses often in Western astrology—most of the planets are named after them!

Astrologers describe the planets as having different "energies." These energies are a lot like the personalities of the deities the planets are named after. Depending on where the planets are in the sky, we feel their energies differently.

The ancient Babylonians gave us the zodiac, which defines the parts of the sky. Like the planets, each part of the zodiac has its own energy. So, when a planet enters a part of the zodiac, their energies mix, and—voilá!—we have a cosmic force that affects life on earth.

The most important part of astrology is you! When you were born, the position of the planets formed what I call your "cosmic fingerprint." It gives us insight into your personality and how you'll react to cosmic forces. One of the most important components of your cosmic fingerprint is your sun sign. Your sun sign is determined by where the sun was positioned in the zodiac when you were born. The sun shines brightly in the sky, and likewise, astrologers believe that your sun sign reflects the essence of your personality. Astrologers use this information to write horoscopes, which are stories about how the cosmos will affect people of each sun sign during a day, week, month, or year.

Once you know your sun sign, you can start to explore your inner universe and join in the tradition of astrology!

Astrology Timeline

Astrology has progressed over time based on scientific discoveries and changes in daily life. On the following pages, we'll explore milestones, movements, and our place in the history of Western astrology.

Prehistory

Before 3000 BCE

Even before humans began documenting events, our ancient ancestors depended on the sun, stars, and moon for survival. They served as our celestial compass for navigation. These first observations of the cosmos laid the foundation for astrology.

Classical Antiquity

800 BCE–500 CE

During this time, astrology was established and widely practiced in the civilizations centered around the Mediterranean Sea.

14,500 BCE, in the area we now call France

Prehistoric people painted over 1,000 images in the Lascaux cave. Recent research suggests these cave paintings may include star charts. Near a painting of a bull is what seems to be a map of the constellation Taurus!

700 BCE, Mesopotamia

The Sumerians and Babylonians established the zodiac and the twelve astrological signs.

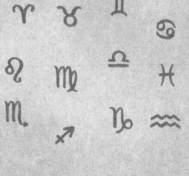

409 BCE, Mesopotamia

The oldest-known horoscope chart was rendered.

Year 1
The Common Era began. The time before this is referred to as BCE or "Before Common Era."

400 BCE, Ancient Greece and Ancient Rome

The Ancient Greeks began developing an extremely rich mythology. It was adopted by the Ancient Romans. This mythology was applied to the planets and the zodiac as astrology developed in the area.

Did You Know? The Ancient Roman emperor Augustus embossed coins with his astrological sign: Capricorn.

Cosmic Challenge: What would your coin look like? Draw it here!

Around year 150, Ancient Greece

Claudius Ptolemy published *Tetrabiblos*. It described how the sun, moon, and planets affected life on earth. Ptolemy explained the planets' personalities and how to calculate horoscopes.

"Mortal as I am, I know that I am born for a day. But when I follow . . . the serried multitude of the stars in their circular course, my feet no longer touch the earth."
—Claudius Ptolemy (100–170)

Islamic Golden Age

700–1450

The Roman Empire collapsed in 476, and the medieval period began in Europe. Few astrological developments were made in Europe at that time. Meanwhile, Muslim civilizations made enormous cultural, economic, and scientific advancements. The scientific discoveries were applied to astrology.

The Renaissance

1300–1650

After the medieval period, art and culture began to flourish in Europe. Interest in astrology picked up, and many philosophers began studying the stars.

973–1050, Ghazni

Al-Biruni, like many scholars of his time, continued to develop astrology, making connections between the stars and math and science in ways we still use today.

1600–1700, England

Astrologers such as William Lilly (1602–1681) focused on developing new systems, like horary astrology, that could be used in everyday life.

Did You Know? Horary is a very specific type of astrology that is used to answer yes-or-no questions.

787–886, Baghdad

Abu Maʿshar wrote practical manuals for training astrologers that have influenced the intellectual history of many cultures.

Did You Know? The Hebrew/Yiddish phrase *mazel tov* ("good luck") derives from the Mishnaic Hebrew word mazzāl, which translates to "constellation" or "destiny."

The Age of Enlightenment

1650–1800

The age of art and culture gave way to the age of reason, science, and rationality across Europe. Scholars became interested in the ancient civilizations of Greece and Rome. They held them up as models for modern society, including their practice of astrology.

1668, England

Sir Isaac Newton created the reflecting telescope, the kind of telescope we use today. It allowed us to see the cosmos more clearly.

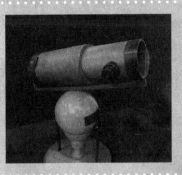

1781, England

Uranus was discovered by William Herschel. At this time, astronomy and astrology became two distinct areas of study. Astronomy emerged as a purely scientific exploration of outer space. Astrology continued as a spiritual tradition.

Romantic Era

1800–1900

There was a huge science and technology boom in Europe and the United States just as the 1800s began. Suddenly we had electricity, photography, and new kinds of transportation. Imaginations were sparked. Stories like *Frankenstein* by Mary Shelley and "The Raven" by Edgar Allen Poe blended ghost stories and science fiction, artists focused on emotion and individualism, and astrology was celebrated as a mystical practice.

Twentieth Century

1900–2000

The century that gave us televisions, computers, and many of the magazines and newspapers we read today also brought Western astrology into popular culture.

1846, Germany

Neptune, the planet associated with spirituality, was discovered.

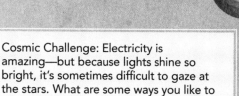

Cosmic Challenge: Electricity is amazing—but because lights shine so bright, it's sometimes difficult to gaze at the stars. What are some ways you like to "unplug"? List them here!

February 18, 1930, United States

Pluto was discovered, and, after that, everyone became obsessed with outer space!

August 24, 1930, England

The first magazine horoscope was published in England by R. H. Naylor.

1968, United States

Astrologer Linda Goodman published her book for adults, *Linda Goodman's Sun Signs*. It was so popular that many believed it started the New Age movement of the 1970s.

The Future of Astrology

2000 and on

Today, new astrologers are using social media to reach more people. They are talking about topics such as gender, race, sexuality, and identity. These fresh faces honor our magical, ancient practice. They also make it fun and easy to understand.

1981, United States

First Lady Nancy Reagan hired Joan Quigley as the official White House astrologer.

Cosmic Challenge: Now, you're part of this timeline, too! Draw a picture or glue a photo of yourself here. What would you like to get out of this guided journey through the stars? Write your goals or intentions below.

1995, United States

Astrologer Susan Miller founded her website, Astrology Zone, where she continues to write detailed, monthly horoscopes for her dedicated readers. Over six million people visit the website each year!

Part One

The Zodiac

What Is the Zodiac?

The zodiac is the lens through which we view the sky. Think of it as a flat map of the sky that wraps around the earth. The map is divided into twelve equal parts, each one representing a section of the sky. In ancient times, civilizations all over the world used the zodiac to track time, from China and Korea to India and Mexico. Each culture labeled the twelve parts of the sky with different animals and symbols.

In Western astrology, the twelve sections are named for the constellations in them: Aries, Taurus, Gemini, Cancer, Leo, Virgo, Libra, Scorpio, Sagittarius, Capricorn, Aquarius, and Pisces. These constellations are what we call the twelve "signs."

The twelve signs are Greek reimaginings based on ancient Babylonian myths from over 5,000 years ago. Over time, astrologers noticed similarities between the signs and other facets of life. These are called "correspondences." Because astrology is so old, certain details have been lost. For example, we don't know why Aries, Leo, and Sagittarius are considered "fire signs," instead of "water signs." But these associations have been observed, studied, and practiced for thousands of years!

Did You Know? *Zodiac* is a Greek word that means "circle of animals."

Cosmic Challenge: In astrology, everything is part of a pattern. Once you understand the rhythm of the pattern, it's easy to start following the stars! What patterns do you see in the zodiac wheel?

_____

_____

Finding Your Sign

Now it's time to start exploring your own cosmic fingerprint!

At the time of your birth, every celestial body was in one zodiac sign or another. When someone asks you "what's your sign," they're specifically asking about the position of the sun at your exact moment of birth. This is your "sun sign," or often called your "star sign."

Your sun sign symbolizes your truth. It's your radiance, essence, and authentic self. It's also what makes you happy and helps you understand your likes and dislikes!

Find where your birthday falls in the following pages to help figure out your sun sign!

MY SUN SIGN IS

_____

Did You Know? People born on the first calendar day of a sign might say they're born on the "cusp" of it. However, astrologers don't use cusps. They don't exist! Based on the zodiac, you're either one sign or the other.

Your Radiance

As you learn all about the twelve signs on the following pages, keep these prompts in mind. Then come back to this page and reflect on what your sun sign means for you. Remember, Cosmic Warrior, no one is perfect. In fact, our blind spots are often what define our unique radiance. How do you shine?

My sun sign is great because:

_____

_____

_____

_____

My sun sign frustrates me because:

_____

_____

_____

_____

The Twelve Zodiac Signs

The twelve signs of the zodiac are core components of astrology. Here's how we interpret their correspondences:

DATES: The calendar days of the year when the sun is in each sign.

ELEMENT: Fire is connected to action and passion. Earth is connected to nature and practicality. Air is connected to ideas and friendship. Water is connected to emotions and creativity.

QUALITY: Cardinal energy is great at starting projects. Fixed energy excels at maintaining systems. Mutable energy propels change.

SYMBOL: This visual representation of the sign connects it to mythology.

Cosmic Challenge: Create a mythological creature to represent you. Combine your favorite animals, symbols, or possessions—let your imagination run wild!

Did You Know? The elements come from ancient philosophers who believed that the entire universe was made of four elements: fire, earth, air, and water.

RULING PLANET: For every sign, there is a planet with similar qualities and energies. These energies go together like peanut butter and jelly! Once you explore a zodiac sign, find its ruling planet in Part Two: The Planets for a deeper dive!

LUCKY DAY: Hundreds of years ago, it was believed that each planet ruled a specific day of the week, and each sign had a ruling planet. So, based on your sun sign, you can figure out which day has good vibes for you.

EXPRESSION: This is a statement that describes the sign's core experience.

COLOR: This is a visual representation of the energy of a sign. This color shares the mood, energy, and spirit of the sign.

PERSONALITY TRAITS: A description of the sign's essence, values, and how the sign responds to different situations.

GOOD DAY: How the personality traits manifest in a positive way.

BAD DAY: How the personality traits manifest in a challenging way.

HIDDEN TALENT: Based on the personality traits of each sign, astrologers can determine a fitting pastime for each sign.

FAST FRIENDS: The personality traits of certain signs go well with those of other signs. People with these signs are likely to get along together.

IN MY ORBIT: Do you know anyone born under this sign? Write their names and birthdays.

Understanding how the astrological energies impact you *personally* is the first step to becoming an astrologer. What energy inspires you? What element attracts you? Write your observations in the margins on the following pages.

DATES
March 21–April 19

ELEMENT
Fire

QUALITY
Cardinal

SYMBOL
The Ram

RULING PLANET
Mars

EXPRESSION
"I am."

COLOR
Red

LUCKY DAY
Tuesday

Aries

PERSONALITY TRAITS: Aries is the first sign of the zodiac. It symbolizes the match that sparks the entire zodiac, so Aries *definitely* know how to get the party started! Aries have a can-do attitude and are known to be impulsive and spontaneous. Aries also have a competitive streak. They love to be number one! They are also brave warriors who will never back down from a challenge, especially if it involves helping others.

GOOD DAY: Passionate, energetic, spontaneous, fearless, playful, brave, independent

BAD DAY: Selfish, bossy, short-tempered, stubborn, competitive

HIDDEN TALENT: Relay racing

FAST FRIENDS: Gemini, Leo, Libra, Sagittarius, Aquarius

IN MY ORBIT: _____

_____

DATES
April 20–May 20

ELEMENT
Earth

QUALITY
Fixed

SYMBOL
The Bull

RULING PLANET
Venus

EXPRESSION
"I have."

COLOR
Pink

LUCKY DAY
Friday

Taurus

PERSONALITY TRAITS: Grounded in reality, earthy Taurus values stability and security. The first earth sign of the zodiac, these celestial bulls are all about honoring their five senses: hearing, touch, taste, sight, and smell. So *obviously*, Taurus loves nice things! It's true that these bulls do have a bit of a stubborn streak. But at the end of the day, their hardheadedness is just a reflection of their incredible loyalty and devotion.

GOOD DAY: Loyal, supportive, logical, careful, dedicated, practical, reliable

BAD DAY: Stubborn, materialistic, confrontational, moody, possessive

HIDDEN TALENT: Cooking

FAST FRIENDS: Cancer, Virgo, Scorpio, Capricorn, Pisces

IN MY ORBIT: _____

_____

DATES
May 21–June 20

ELEMENT
Air

QUALITY
Mutable

SYMBOL
The Twins

RULING PLANET
Mercury

EXPRESSION
"I think."

COLOR
Yellow

LUCKY DAY
Wednesday

Gemini

PERSONALITY TRAITS: Have you ever been so busy, you wished you could duplicate yourself to accomplish everything on your to-do list? That's *exactly* the spirit of Gemini! Symbolized by the twins, Gemini are curious creatures who are driven by their interests. These twins love to chat, so you can always find playful Gemini drifting between birthday parties, friend groups, and afterschool activities. In fact, this air sign is so busy, it's easy for Gemini to become a bit flaky. But Gemini don't mean any harm. They're simply trying to have fun!

GOOD DAY: Intelligent, communicative, curious, silly, creative, adaptable, adventurous

BAD DAY: Flaky, unpredictable, inconsistent, indecisive, nervous

HIDDEN TALENT: Songwriting

FAST FRIENDS: Aries, Leo, Libra, Sagittarius, Aquarius

IN MY ORBIT: _____

_____

DATES
June 21–July 22

ELEMENT
Water

QUALITY
Cardinal

SYMBOL
The Crab
or Crustacean

RULING PLANET
Moon

EXPRESSION
"I feel."

COLOR
Silver

LUCKY DAY
Monday

Cancer

PERSONALITY TRAITS: Cancers have a nurturing and protective spirit. They love to take care of their friends and loved ones, and are especially passionate about tending to plants and animals. Since building a supportive environment is important to them, sometimes Cancers can become a bit possessive. It's hard for them to let go of what they love! However, once these celestial crustaceans feel safe, they will be sure to *always* have your back.

GOOD DAY: Sensitive, nurturing, thoughtful, affectionate, loyal, caretaking, artistic

BAD DAY: Moody, defensive, suspicious, manipulative, crabby

HIDDEN TALENT: Surfing

FAST FRIENDS: Taurus, Virgo, Scorpio, Capricorn, Pisces

IN MY ORBIT: _____

_____

DATES
July 23–August 22

ELEMENT
Fire

QUALITY
Fixed

SYMBOL
The Lion

RULING PLANET
Sun

EXPRESSION
"I will."

COLOR
Gold

LUCKY DAY
Sunday

Leo

PERSONALITY TRAITS: Roll out the red carpet—Leo has arrived! These celestial lions are zodiac royalty, and they're *proud* to wear the crowns. They love to bask in the spotlight. They're natural performers! Of course, it's not always easy for Leos to share the stage, so sometimes, they can become a little bit too self-obsessed. But, as long as Leo's name is on the billboard, the wildcats are sure to be dedicated, warm, and supportive friends.

GOOD DAY: Performative, passionate, optimistic, warm, protective, ambitious, friendly

BAD DAY: Jealous, dramatic, proud, dominating, self-centered

HIDDEN TALENT: Karaoke

FAST FRIENDS: Aries, Gemini, Libra, Sagittarius, Aquarius

IN MY ORBIT: _____

_____

DATES
August 23–
September 22

ELEMENT
Earth

QUALITY
Mutable

SYMBOL
The Maiden

RULING PLANET
Mercury

EXPRESSION
"I organize."

COLOR
Orange

LUCKY DAY
Wednesday

Virgo

PERSONALITY TRAITS: Virgos are extremely thoughtful. Smart and witty, this earth sign loves to categorize, organize, and problem-solve. When their attention to detail goes too far, however, Virgo can become a bit critical and nitpicky. But at the end of the day, Virgos love to be helpful. Whether you need help with chores or simply a shoulder to cry on, Virgo is always ready to offer support.

GOOD DAY: Intelligent, analytical, practical, thoughtful, organized, logical, helpful

BAD DAY: Nervous, paranoid, idealistic, critical, apprehensive

HIDDEN TALENT: Computer programming

FAST FRIENDS: Taurus, Cancer, Scorpio, Capricorn, Pisces

IN MY ORBIT: _____

_____

DATES
September 23–
October 22

ELEMENT
Air

QUALITY
Cardinal

SYMBOL
The Scales

RULING PLANET
Venus

EXPRESSION
"I balance."

COLOR
Green

LUCKY DAY
Friday

Libra

PERSONALITY TRAITS: As the only inanimate object of the zodiac, Libra has a big job! Symbolized by the scales, Libras are all about creating balance and harmony. But not everything is always evenly distributed, and sometimes it's difficult for this air sign to make up its mind. When push comes to shove, however, Libras will always choose peace and harmony. That's why they're so interested in the creative arts!

GOOD DAY: Elegant, fair, diplomatic, sociable, charming, agreeable, peaceful

BAD DAY: Indirect, evasive, vain, judgmental, opportunistic

HIDDEN TALENT: Photography

FAST FRIENDS: Aries, Gemini, Leo, Sagittarius, Aquarius

IN MY ORBIT: _____

_____

DATES
October 23–
November 21

ELEMENT
Water

QUALITY
Fixed

SYMBOL
The Scorpion

RULING PLANET
Pluto

EXPRESSION
"I desire."

COLOR
Black

LUCKY DAY
Tuesday

Scorpio

PERSONALITY TRAITS: As a water sign, Scorpios are extremely connected to their emotions. However, this mysterious sign is also known for its powerful, venomous stinger. But Scorpios need to be sure they don't end up poking the wrong person: They can let their emotions get the best of them. At the end of the day, however, this water sign is extremely loyal, hardworking, and relentlessly ambitious.

GOOD DAY: Magnetic, dedicated, deep, discerning, ambitious, mysterious

BAD DAY: Controlling, obsessive, jealous, stubborn, bitter

HIDDEN TALENT: Detective work

FAST FRIENDS: Taurus, Cancer, Virgo, Capricorn, Pisces

IN MY ORBIT: _____

_____

DATES
November 22–
December 21

ELEMENT
Fire

QUALITY
Mutable

SYMBOL
The Archer

RULING PLANET
Jupiter

EXPRESSION
"I discover."

COLOR
Blue

LUCKY DAY
Thursday

Sagittarius

PERONALITY TRAITS: The last fire sign of the zodiac, Sagittarius is on a *serious* adventure. Symbolized by the archer, Sagittarians are known to propel their arrow long distances, leading them to explore different ideas, philosophies, and even destinations! Just like a wildfire, it's impossible to contain Sagittarians' energy. Sometimes, these celestial archers can end up scorching even their closest friends! But so long as they have room to roam, Sagittarians are sure to be the life of *every* party.

GOOD DAY: Humorous, philosophical, adventurous, communicative, engaging, clever

BAD DAY: Indulgent, impatient, careless, boastful, righteous

HIDDEN TALENT: Archaeology

FAST FRIENDS: Aries, Gemini, Leo, Libra, Aquarius

IN MY ORBIT: _____

_____

DATES
December 22–
January 19

ELEMENT
Earth

QUALITY
Cardinal

SYMBOL
The Sea-Goat

RULING PLANET
Saturn

EXPRESSION
"I build."

COLOR
Black

LUCKY DAY
Saturday

Capricorn

PERSONALITY TRAITS: Symbolized by the sea-goat (a mystical creature with the body of a goat and the tail of a fish), Capricorns can navigate both land and water. These hardworking earth signs are experts at fusing their hard work with their intuition. Because they're big-picture thinkers who are always aspiring to achieve greatness, Capricorns can sometimes be a bit harsh or insensitive. But it's worth it in the end. These celestial sea-goats will always inspire others to reach their fullest potential.

GOOD DAY: Enterprising, resourceful, honest, determined, diligent, responsible, mature

BAD DAY: Unemotional, cold, rigid, harsh, pessimistic

HIDDEN TALENT: Filmmaking

FAST FRIENDS: Taurus, Cancer, Virgo, Scorpio, Pisces

IN MY ORBIT: _____

_____

DATES
January 20–
February 18

ELEMENT
Air

QUALITY
Fixed

SYMBOL
The Water-Bearer

RULING PLANET
Uranus

EXPRESSION
"I innovate."

COLOR
Purple

LUCKY DAY
Saturday

Aquarius

PERSONALITY TRAITS: Although Aquarius is often mistaken for a water sign, it's actually the last air sign of the zodiac. Symbolized by the generous water-bearer, Aquarians care deeply about bestowing life upon the land. Aquarians are humanitarians, revolutionaries, and freethinkers. Because they're so rebellious, it's easy for this air sign to become a bit righteous from time to time. But Aquarians want to change the world—and they're not afraid to do whatever it takes to innovate and progress.

GOOD DAY: Humanitarian, independent, revolutionary, free-thinking, eccentric

BAD DAY: Aloof, contrary, detached, judgmental, stubborn

HIDDEN TALENT: Costume design

FAST FRIENDS: Aries, Gemini, Leo, Libra, Sagittarius

IN MY ORBIT: _____

_____

DATES
February 19–
March 20

ELEMENT
Water

QUALITY
Mutable

SYMBOL
The Fish

RULING PLANET
Neptune

EXPRESSION
"I dream."

COLOR
Turquoise

LUCKY DAY
Thursday

Pisces

PERSONALITY TRAITS: The last sign of the zodiac, Pisces have absorbed all the lessons of the previous signs—the joys, pains, hopes, and fears. Likewise, these celestial fish are *extremely* sensitive creatures. In fact, they're the most psychic sign of the zodiac! It's easy for Pisces to become overwhelmed, and when they are, they'll be sure to quickly swim away. When this sign stays in place by treading water, however, Pisces are among the most mystical, creative, and artistic of the zodiac.

GOOD DAY: Creative, imaginative, kind, empathic, dreamy, spiritual, mystical

BAD DAY: Escapist, disconnected, flighty, vulnerable, overly sensitive

HIDDEN TALENT: Telepathy

FAST FRIENDS: Taurus, Cancer, Virgo, Scorpio, Capricorn

IN MY ORBIT: _____

_____

Your Co-Stars

Our ancient ancestors would observe how patterns in the sky corresponded to events on earth. You can do this, too, by keeping track of your relationships. Write the names of people in your orbit below.

	Aries	Taurus	Gemini	Cancer	Leo	Virgo
Family	♈	♉	♊	♋	♌	♍
Friends	♈	♉	♊	♋	♌	♍
Pets	♈	♉	♊	♋	♌	♍
Teachers	♈	♉	♊	♋	♌	♍
Crushes	♈	♉	♊	♋	♌	♍
Role Models	♈	♉	♊	♋	♌	♍

How can you use what you've learned to show empathy to people in your life? For example, my best friend is a Capricorn. She is happiest when things are real and concrete, so I'll stop being wishy-washy about plans with her!

_____

_____

_____

Libra	Scorpio	Sagittarius	Capricorn	Aquarius	Pisces

Your Secret Sign

The universe is vast, expansive, and often unpredictable. Similarly, you may discover that you identify with a certain zodiac sign *even* if it's not your sun sign. I call these "secret signs." Maybe you feel connected to this sign emotionally, or maybe you tend to gravitate toward this sign in love or friendship. Every single person is complex, so your secret sign can help you continue to understand your personal dimensionality.

Take this quiz to find out your secret sign. You can also quiz your friends to find out how your secret signs align!

1. At a party, I'm usually:
   a. The center of attention.
   b. Checking out the snacks.
   c. Bouncing between friend groups.
   d. Having a deep, one-on-one conversation.

2. My friends describe me as:
   a. Energetic.
   b. Loyal.
   c. Intelligent.
   d. Sensitive.

3. If my feelings are hurt, I usually:
   a. Try not to get too angry, but I feel the fire burning inside!
   b. Try to ignore it—maybe it will go away.
   c. Shift my perspective and try to understand another point of view.
   d. Grab a tissue: Tears will start rolling down my cheeks!

4. My favorite place is:
   a. The stage.
   b. Near my best friends.
   c. The movie theater.
   d. My bedroom.

5. My favorite season is:
   a. Summer.
   b. Spring.
   c. Fall.
   d. Winter.

6. Pick a color:
   a. Shades of red.
   b. Shades of green.
   c. Shades of yellow.
   d. Shades of blue.

7. When I have a crush, I usually:
   a. Make it very public.
   b. Figure out if the feelings are mutual.
   c. Get juicy info on that person from my friends.
   d. Don't tell anyone.

8. The perfect Friday night always includes:
   a. Trying something new and exciting.
   b. Resting after a long week.
   c. Chatting with my friends all night.
   d. Lots of drama—probably involving crushes, too.

9. I get angry when:
   a. I come in last place.
   b. I feel betrayed.
   c. I feel left out.
   d. I feel misunderstood.

10. If I could go on any adventure,
    it would include:
   a. An airplane ticket.
   b. A map.
   c. A partner in crime.
   d. A dream journal.

11. I spend a lot of time thinking about:
   a. Becoming famous.
   b. Succeeding in school.
   c. Friends, family, and crushes.
   d. The mysteries of life.

12. When I think about a forest, I feel:
   a. Spooked.
   b. Enchanted.
   c. Claustrophobic.
   d. Inspired.

Give yourself the following points for each answer: a = 1; b = 2; c = 3; d = 4

Total points: _____

Find your total points in the key below to discover your secret sign!

KEY

12-14 POINTS Aries	30-32 POINTS Taurus
15-17 POINTS Leo	33-35 POINTS Virgo
18-20 POINTS Sagittarius	36-38 POINTS Capricorn
21-23 POINTS Gemini	39-41 POINTS Cancer
24-26 POINTS Libra	42-44 POINTS Scorpio
27-29 POINTS Aquarius	45-48 POINTS Pisces

My secret sign is _____.

Part Two

The Planets

What Are the Planets?

Now that you know all about the zodiac, let's start adding even more dimensionality!

In astrology, we track the movement of the celestial bodies as they appear to us, looking up at the sky from the earth's surface. A planet is a celestial body that we see moving through the earth's sky in a regular pattern. Our ancient ancestors didn't know the different types of celestial bodies that exist in outer space. "Planet" means "wanderer" in Greek. This term was used to identify the most important cosmic objects. That includes the sun, the moon, and Pluto!

Although they're not always visible, we can count on the celestial bodies' movements across the cosmos. Our ancient ancestors studied the planets' movements and realized that each planet was associated with a particular theme or aspect of life. In a way, you can think of each planet as having its own unique job. We often describe that job as the planet's energy or role.

At any particular moment, each planet is occupying a zodiac sign. A planet's job doesn't change, but it's influenced by the zodiac sign it travels across. For instance, Mercury is always the planet of communication. However, this communication is going to differ if Mercury is in fiery Aries or secretive Scorpio.

In astrology, a planet's orbit is its movement through all twelve zodiac signs. The moon takes approximately 28 days to complete an orbit, whereas it takes Pluto 248 years. That's 90,520 days!

The planets with shorter orbits, also called the personal planets, have a greater impact on our day-to-day life because they are closer to the earth. In fact, we can see them without a telescope. These planets directly influence our routines, activities, and communication.

On the other hand, the planets with longer orbits, also called the outer planets, have a powerful long-term influence. Because they are farther away from the earth, we won't necessarily feel them every day but rather over long stretches of time. The outer planets are connected to our future jobs, hopes, and aspirations.

Cosmic Challenge: Mercury, Venus, Mars, Jupiter, and Saturn are visible for much of the year with the naked eye. Can you spot these bright celestial bodies among the stars like our ancestors did?

The Ten Planets

Each planet has different associations. Here's a little more insight into what some of the most important categories mean:

CHANGES ZODIAC SIGN: When a planet makes a complete orbit, it goes through all twelve signs of the zodiac. It's important to know how frequently a planet changes signs.

RULES: Each planet corresponds with a zodiac sign, and in some cases, two! This system was first established by the ancient Greeks thousands of years ago.

KEYWORD: You can look to this keyword to understand the essence of the planet. Use this term as a reference!

FUNCTION: Each planet has a very specific function in the zodiac, which links the planet to certain topics and themes. By learning about the function of each planet, you can discover why certain astrological events are associated with particular occurrences in your own life.

MYTHOLOGY: In Western astrology, all the planets are named after Greek and Roman gods or goddesses. Likewise, the mythology of these deities is applied to the planets. In a way, the planets embody these mythological figures.

PERSONAL REFLECTION: As you learn about each planet, write what its keyword means to you. Does it bring up aspects of yourself you'd like to work on or celebrate?

Ready to learn more about the planets? Let's blast off!

Cosmic Challenge: If you were to create a planet, what would it be named? What is its function? What does it look like? Draw and caption it here!

_____

The Sun

CHANGES ZODIAC SIGN
About every 30 days

RULES
Leo

KEYWORD
Truth

FUNCTION: The sun symbolizes your fundamental essence. Likewise, it governs the ego, sense of self, and external realities. The sun shines light on the truth, so this celestial body is associated with honesty and authenticity.

MYTHOLOGY: The sun's illumination has always been sacred. In fact, the sun has been celebrated since the dawn of humanity. It is our life force, our essence. Its dependable warmth and light facilitate growth. It is often personified as a deity. A few examples are Ra in Ancient Egyptian culture, Apollo in Classical Antiquity, or Surya in Hinduism.

PERSONAL TRUTH:

_____

_____

The Moon

CHANGES ZODIAC SIGN
About every 2.5 days

RULES
Cancer

KEYWORD
Emotions

FUNCTION: Each day, our activities are guided by the sun. At night, however, the moon comes up and reflects the sun. The moon asks how we *feel* about everything that happened to us over the course of the day. In other words, the moon governs our emotional inner world and how we feel about situations. It's what we experience internally, helping us understand what makes us feel safe, protected, and secure.

MYTHOLOGY: In Classical Antiquity, the moon was associated with several female deities: Luna, Diana, Artemis, Juno, and Selene. Each goddess was assigned to one of the moon's phases. They all had very different personalities, symbolizing the moon's changing disposition as it transformed in the sky.

PERSONAL EMOTIONS:

_____

_____

Mercury

CHANGES ZODIAC SIGN
About every 14 days

RULES
Virgo and Gemini

KEYWORD
Communication

FUNCTION: Mercury governs our communication and expression. Mercury works with the other planets to help make sense of abstract concepts, including our emotions and desires. Rational and organized, Mercury is motivated by its curiosity.

MYTHOLOGY: In Roman mythology, Mercury served as the divine messenger. Wearing winged sandals, Mercury delivered messages between gods and mortals, as well as the living and the dead. Mercury was playful—and sometimes mischievous. Depending on who he partnered with, he would be either naughty or nice.

PERSONAL COMMUNICATION:

_____

_____

Venus

CHANGES ZODIAC SIGN	RULES	KEYWORD
About every 4-5 weeks	Taurus and Libra	Desire

FUNCTION: In astrology, Venus represents our idealized version of love and our perception of value. Venusian energy is passionate, romantic, and all about beauty, appearances, and the way things look. Venus wants to eat sweets, be fanned with palms, and oiled up with expensive beauty products—but sometimes these indulgences can go a bit too far. After all, too much chocolate always leads to a tummyache! When it comes to Venus, it's important to practice moderation.

MYTHOLOGY: One of the most well-known Roman goddesses, Venus is the symbol of love, money, and abundance. Although these attributes are generally perceived as positive, Venus also has a dark side. She could also be vain and indulgent, choosing to satisfy her immediate desires instead of long-term happiness.

PERSONAL DESIRE:

_____

_____

Mars

CHANGES ZODIAC SIGN	RULES	KEYWORD
About every 6-7 weeks	Aries	Action

FUNCTION: Mars is fueled by adrenaline, so this planet governs our determination and drive. Action-oriented, Mars's energy manifests when we're racing to meet a deadline, running to catch a bus, or competing for a prize. Mars is energetic and enterprising, propelling motivation and forward movement.

MYTHOLOGY: Ares, the Greek god of war, was depicted as violent and aggressive. However, Mars, his Roman counterpart, was strategic and dignified. In Roman mythology, Mars governed military conquests and soldiers, as well as agriculture and farmers. Mars was the mascot of the Roman Empire. Mars's symbol, a circle with a pointed arrow, represented the god's spear and shield. Over time, it was adopted as the male symbol.

PERSONAL ACTION:

_____

_____

Jupiter

CHANGES ZODIAC SIGN
About every 12-13 months

RULES
Sagittarius

KEYWORD
Expansion

FUNCTION: This gas giant is larger than life in both size and attitude. Jupiter symbolizes expansion, so this planet enlarges everything that comes into its orbit. Jupiter can be very lucky—who wouldn't want the planet of expansion smiling on fortune? But Jupiter can also make a difficult situation worse. Everything is amplified under Jupiter's influence: the good, the bad, and the ugly.

MYTHOLOGY: It's no surprise that the largest planet in the solar system is named after the head honcho of Classical Antiquity. More commonly, he is known by his Greek name, Zeus. In Greek and Roman mythology, Jupiter overthrew his tyrannical father, Saturn, and seized power. Then Jupiter divided the universe into three realms that he shared with his brothers: Jupiter ruled the heavens, Neptune governed the sea, and Pluto oversaw the Underworld.

PERSONAL EXPANSION:

_____

_____

Saturn

CHANGES ZODIAC SIGN
About every 2.5 years

RULES
Capricorn

KEYWORD
Responsibility

FUNCTION: In astrology, the planet Saturn is connected to rules, responsibilities, and restrictions. Stern and serious, Saturn is often seen as the opposite of jolly Jupiter. Saturn is all work, no play. But despite Saturn's stoic disposition, this planet's "tough love" is important. Saturn helps us become emotionally stronger, fostering bravery and compassion.

MYTHOLOGY: Before Zeus reigned over the cosmos, Saturn ruled the universe as the king of gods. But he was too power hungry. Literally. Saturn was so tyrannical that he actually ate his children as an attempt to stay on the throne. Eventually, however, his disturbing behavior caught up with him. In the end, he was overthrown by his son, Jupiter, who forced him to regurgitate the others, Neptune and Pluto. Saturn learned his lessons the hard way. By becoming so obsessed with power, Saturn ended up creating the very reality he feared the most.

PERSONAL RESPONSIBILITY:

_____

_____

Uranus

CHANGES ZODIAC SIGN
About every 7 years

RULES
Aquarius

KEYWORD
Innovation

FUNCTION: Wise and discerning, Uranus symbolizes revolution, rebellion, and innovation. Uranian energy encourages us to break free of stale traditions and embrace the unknown. Although Uranus can be a bit destructive at times, its nonconformist ways help spark ideas that propel progress. Forget the past! Uranus is all about the future.

MYTHOLOGY: Uranus, a very ancient deity, was actually the *first* king of the gods. Uranus wasn't a big fan of his title though. He knew that the ruling powers were flawed. When Uranus was overthrown by his son, Saturn, he moved into the deeper realms of the sky, watching over the heavens with wisdom.

PERSONAL INNOVATION:

_____

_____

Did You Know? Uranus is unusual. It's the first planet discovered by a telescope, the only celestial body named after a Greek deity, and is tilted so far on its axis—a whopping 98-degree angle.

Neptune

CHANGES ZODIAC SIGN
About every 14 years

RULES
Pisces

KEYWORD
Intuition

FUNCTION: In astrology, water is associated with emotions, intuition, and psychic powers. Likewise, the planet Neptune is associated with the subconscious realm. On a good day, Neptune is empathetic, creative, and spiritual—a gentle, magical mist. On a bad day, however, Neptune can be a dense, thick fog, making it hard to tell the difference between fantasy and reality. Neptune can be both a dream and a nightmare.

MYTHOLOGY: Neptune's childhood wasn't easy. He and his brother, Pluto, were eaten by their father, Saturn. After years in Saturn's stomach, he was finally released by his other brother, Jupiter. Neptune was then forced to rule the ocean. His responsibility was great—the water world is massive! But Neptune was frequently frustrated by his position as god of the sea. He was notorious for throwing temper tantrums that would *truly* make a splash.

PERSONAL INTUITION:

_____

_____

Pluto

CHANGES ZODIAC SIGN
About every 14-30 years

RULES
Scorpio

KEYWORD
Transformation

FUNCTION: Like its mythological namesake, Pluto governs our secrets and undercover information. Pluto exposes the areas of life that require total and complete transformation. Plutonian energy can sometimes be controlling or manipulative, but fundamentally, this mysterious planet reminds us that there are many things in life we cannot control. When in doubt, don't be afraid to let go.

MYTHOLOGY: Pluto, also known as Hades, was the god of the Underworld, the judge of the dead, and the ruler of wealth. Both freedom and fortune were found in the Underworld, so Pluto's domain was intense and powerful. In terms of temperament, Pluto wasn't particularly volatile, but he did know how to hold a grudge.

PERSONAL TRANSFORMATION:

_____

_____

Planetary Knowledge

Now that you've met the planets, find out how well you know their sensibilities. Challenge your astrology skills with this quiz!

1. Of the following four, which two planets help you finish your work?

   a. Venus
   b. Mars
   c. Saturn
   d. Neptune

2. Of the following four, which two planets love to socialize?

   a. Mercury
   b. Jupiter
   c. Uranus
   d. Pluto

3. Of the following four, which planet is most likely to lie?

   a. Sun
   b. Moon
   c. Mercury
   d. Mars

4. Of the following four, which two planets love decorating?

   a. Venus
   b. Mars
   c. Neptune
   d. Pluto

Your Ruling Planet

Based on my sun sign, _____,

I'm connected to the planet _____.

Now that you've identified your planet, consider ways you can harness its energy. Brainstorm some ideas here!

_____

_____

_____

_____

_____

_____

_____

_____

_____

_____

_____

_____

Safe Space

Song lyrics.

Thoughts on the universe.

A self-portrait.

The scariest monster.

Blueprints of your dream house.

A delicious recipe.

Favorite outfit.

Poetry.

Secrets.

Everyone expresses themselves differently. This is your safe space to get creative. Use what you've learned about the cosmos to help you brainstorm artistic projects, work through challenging emotions, or plan for the future. Use the ideas in the margins as a launching pad, or come up with your own ideas!

Future aspirations.

To-do lists.

A fancy car.

Childhood memories.

Stickers.

Abstract shapes.

Magic spells.

Angers or frustrations.

Powerful robot.

Part Three

The Cosmos in Motion

What Are Cosmic Events?

Astrology is ancient, but its practice isn't stuck in time. The planets are always in motion, and likewise, different astrological events are always occurring. They provide more dimensionality to the cosmic forces at work upon us. When you observe the celestial bodies overhead, you can apply your astrology skills to anticipate changes in your life.

Have you ever read your horoscope? Maybe you've wondered what astrologers use to create their cosmic interpretations—especially when their predictions turn out to be accurate!

Astrologers use a special table called an "ephemeris" to write horoscopes. Organized by date, an ephemeris lists the placement of every single planet in the zodiac. Astrologers use this tool to look at past, present, and future dates, creating predictions based on the ways the planets connect with one another in the sky.

Many cosmic events can be predicted and observed without an ephemeris. In this section, we'll explore how those events affect you.

Cosmic Challenge: In folklore, werewolves transform under full moons, a common cosmic event. But as you'll find out on the next pages, the full moon only reveals what is already there: the good, the bad, and the ugly. Here, draw your werewolf self. Don't be afraid to make it scary!

The Lunar Cycle

Over the course of a month, the moon is visible to us in many different forms. It emerges as a bright sphere during the full moon phase, appears in diverse crescent shapes during its waxing and waning phases, and then is entirely invisible during the new moon phase.

The moon takes approximately 28 days to complete its cycle. During this time, it affects our emotional ups and downs.

Regardless of its position overhead, the moon always stays close to the earth. It's our cosmic companion. Sometimes, even in the daylight, we can see the outline of the moon—a reminder of its dependability. Think about how the gravitational force of the moon influences the ocean's tides. As the moon moves around the earth, it pulls large amounts of water toward it, creating high and low tides. It's pretty incredible!

Each moon phase has different associations. Here's a little more insight into what some of the most important categories mean:

OCCURRENCE: Write the date this phase begins.

KEYWORD: As you continue learning about the moon, you can look to this keyword to understand the essence of its lunar phase. Use this term as a reference!

ENERGY: During each phase, the moon emits a particular energy. When you observe the phases of the moon, you can work with this energy to help propel forward motion. For instance, based on the moon, you can figure out the best time to start or complete a project.

MY REFLECTION: As each phase comes around, harness its energy and note the effects. Try to begin this reflection activity during the next New Moon. It's going to be a powerful month for you!

Reflecting the sun's light, each of the moon's phases offer a different way of looking at our lives. Let's explore them!

Cosmic Challenge: Use the calendar to begin your observations. What phase is the moon in right now? Draw what the phase looks like, write the date, the lunar phase, and what energy you're feeling under this moon.

date: _____ month: _____ year: _____

lunar phase: _____

energy: _____

_____

_____

_____

Cosmic Challenge: Have you ever made a wish over birthday candles or tossed a lucky penny into a fountain? These are small manifestations. You can even call them spells! Try one during the new moon.

New Moon

next occurrence : _____

KEYWORD: Reflection

ENERGY: When the sun and moon are in the same sign, the moon is in its New Moon phase. During this lunation, the moon is not illuminated. The night is at its darkest. Our ancestors used these periods to stay indoors and reflect. Many of our best creative ideas occur during the New Moon phase. This is a great time to set intentions to manifest change.

MY IDEAS:

_____

_____

_____

Waxing Crescent

next occurrence : _____

KEYWORD: Breakthrough

ENERGY: During the Waxing Crescent phase, the moon appears as a sliver, indicating the beginning of something new and exciting. As we push through the darkness, we move past complacency and are inspired to take action.

MY INTENTION:

_____

_____

_____

First Quarter

next occurrence : _____

KEYWORD: Building

ENERGY: When the moon is in the First Quarter phase, we see 50 percent of its illumination. During this time, we continue moving toward our goals. This is the time for planning and organizing.

MY PLAN:

Waxing Gibbous

next occurrence : _____

KEYWORD: Perfecting

ENERGY: The moon appears to be almost full during the Waxing Gibbous phase. Under this lunation, we take our intentions to the next level by adding even more layers of dimensionality. During the Waxing Gibbous phase, we begin to challenge, question, and ask "why." There is a curiosity embedded within this moon.

MY QUESTIONS:

Full Moon

KEYWORD: Awareness

ENERGY: A Full Moon is the climax of the lunar cycle. It occurs when the moon and sun are in direct opposition. During this phase, there is maximum illumination and the night sky is electrified by the moon's radiance. The Full Moon shines light on everything, so important discoveries are often made during this lunation where we have complete perspective.

MY DISCOVERIES:

_____

_____

_____

Waning Gibbous

KEYWORD: Communication

ENERGY: A shadow begins to creep across the moon's face as it enters the next lunation. During the Waning Gibbous phase, we share the information that was revealed during the Full Moon phase. Given this new insight, we connect with our community and solidify plans. Now, thanks to the support of others, our goals become realized.

MY SUPPORT SYSTEM:

_____

_____

_____

Last Quarter

next occurrence : _____

KEYWORD: Readjustment

ENERGY: The moon returns to 50 percent illumination in the second to last lunation. We accomplish our goals during the Waning Gibbous phase, so during the Last Quarter phase, we sit back, relax, and watch the results of our efforts unfold.

MY ACHIEVEMENTS:

Waning Crescent

next occurrence : _____

KEYWORD: Closure

ENERGY: The lunar cycle concludes with the Waning Crescent, a sliver of light on a darkening moon. By now, all work has been done, and what we've worked on no longer exists in its original form. Under this dark sky, we're inspired to reflect on our growth. This is an excellent time to process, think about our experiences, and practice self-care.

MY REFLECTIONS:

Did You Know? Whether self-care means listening to music, taking a bubble bath, or having an honest conversation with a close friend, this routine is something that makes you feel good. Indulge in self-care during this phase!

Eclipses

Eclipses happen when the earth, sun, and moon are all aligned in the sky. The blocked light creates magnificent shadows and silhouettes that are visible from the earth.

Ancient civilizations believed that eclipses were signals of danger. Quite specifically, they believed eclipses meant the apocalypse was coming. Although we no longer connect eclipses to end days, astrologically speaking, eclipses are still a very big deal!

> Did You Know?
> The apocalypse is the final destruction of the world described differently by world religions.

From an astrological point of view, eclipses speed up time by propelling the inevitable. For instance, if tension has been brewing with a friend, you may find that you decide to part ways during the eclipse. In this way, eclipses open new doors by slamming others shut. We often find abrupt and sudden shifts occuring during these cosmic events. Though the shifts can sometimes be harsh, eclipses help us get closer to achieving goals and aspirations!

You may be surprised to discover that eclipses are actually not *that* rare. Each year, there are between three and seven eclipses, which often occur in clusters. But, eclipses can only be seen at specific places and times. It is *very* special when you do get to witness one of these cosmic occurrences with your own eyes!

There are two different types of eclipses: solar and lunar. Let's explore the cosmic differences between these two.

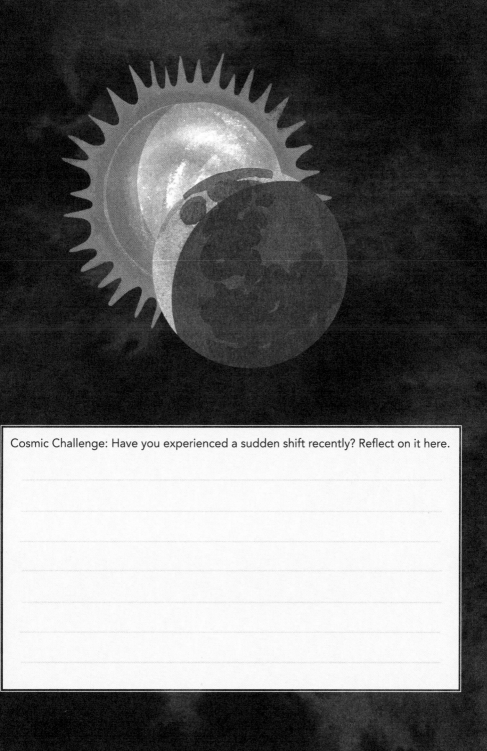

Cosmic Challenge: Have you experienced a sudden shift recently? Reflect on it here.

Solar

Solar eclipses occur during the New Moon phase when the sun and moon align in the same zodiac sign. In this configuration, the moon passes between the sun and earth—and if this occurs during daylight, the result is breathtaking. For several moments, the sun is completely blocked by the moon's silhouette.

Solar eclipses correspond with new beginnings and unexpected opportunities. Since the sun, which symbolizes our external experience, is hidden by the moon, which represents our emotional inner world, a solar eclipse can be very emotional. For many people, solar eclipses are when we realize we need more than what we have, and we send wishes to the universe to welcome abundance.

Cosmic Challenge: What would you like to receive in abundance? Is it an object? A feeling? An achievement?

_____

_____

_____

Did You Know? The shadow cast by a celestial body is known as its "umbra."

Lunar

Lunar eclipses occur during the Full Moon phase. But, unlike a normal full moon that reflects the sun's light, the moon here reflects the earth's shadow during the lunar eclipse. With the earth perfectly wedged between the sun and moon, the moon appears to have a rusty, red tone—this distinctive hue is why lunar eclipses are often referred to as "blood moons."

As the moon reflects the earth's umbra, it allows us to see the truth of a situation through a different lens. With this awareness, you can let go of whatever is no longer making you happy. This is the time to say goodbye. Letting go is hard, remember, but everything is cyclical. Endings always occur before new beginnings.

Cosmic Challenge: What would you like to let go of? Frustration? Self-doubt? An old toy?

_____

_____

Retrogrades

Ancient stargazers observed an interesting phenomenon. Every now and then, the planets would stop, pivot, and begin moving backward in the sky. When a planet did this, our ancestors observed that its functions would also be skewed during this time. We call this a retrograde orbit.

Planets don't actually move backward. Retrograde motion is an optical illusion! Imagine passing a car on the highway: For a moment, the other car may appear to drift backward. This is exactly what happens in the sky when a planet goes retrograde. When planets appear to reverse, our perspective changes from what it had been prior. Things are a little bit off!

Did You Know? A planet is not "in" retrograde; a planet "is" retrograde.

Each planet's retrograde is different. Here's what we'll cover for each planet:

FREQUENCY: This is how often a planet's retrograde orbit occurs. As you'll see, some planets go backward much more frequently than others!

LENGTH: This is how long a planet remains retrograde. During this time, we can expect some shifts to occur.

IMPACT: This is how strongly we'll notice the retrograde. The strength of the impact depends on how often the planet goes in reverse. As you'll see, some planets spend almost half of their orbit retrograde, so their backward spins don't affect us very heavily.

MEANING: This is how a particular planet's retrograde will impact life on earth. Some impacts are easy to observe. For example, Mercury retrograde screws up travel. Other impacts are much more emotional or internal.

ADVICE: This is how I suggest you prepare for or deal with a retrograde orbit.

PLAN: Write your own ideas on how you specifically should deal with this planet's retrograde.

Let's explore these cosmic reversals . . . hang on tight!

Mercury

FREQUENCY: Every 3 or 4 months

LENGTH: About 21 days

IMPACT: High

MEANING: Mercury is the messenger planet, so when it is retrograde, all transmitters are impacted. You should expect frustrating miscommunications, technology meltdowns, and travel delays.

ADVICE: Make sure to read the fine print, give yourself lots of extra travel time, and don't be afraid to repeat yourself if you feel misunderstood!

PLAN:

Venus

FREQUENCY: Every 18 months

LENGTH: About 40 days

IMPACT: High

MEANING: Venus is the planet of love and beauty. So, when it backtracks in the sky, our romantic relationships may be impacted. Expect lots of unexpected breakups and surprising makeups during this time. Venus also governs our values, so your concept of "worth" may be compromised under this sky. You may value objects, yourself, and everything differently.

ADVICE: Be mindful of your heart during this time: When it comes to love, you may be led astray. Also, avoid making any radical shifts in your appearance during this time. A simple haircut has the potential to turn into a total disaster!

PLAN:

Mars

FREQUENCY: Every 26 months

LENGTH: About 70 days

IMPACT: High

MEANING: Mars is action and determination. So, when this high-octane planet goes backward, it's hard to get things done! Instead of feeling accomplished and productive, we may turn our anger inward. We may feel stressed and dissatisfied. We may misdirect our frustration as our behavior becomes increasingly passive-aggressive.

ADVICE: Patience is key during Mars retrograde. You may not see the effects of your work until this retrograde ends, so don't be too hard on yourself. This is a great time to reflect on your goals and ambitions and carve out space for observation.

PLAN:

Jupiter

FREQUENCY: Once per year

LENGTH: About 120 days

IMPACT: Medium

MEANING: During Jupiter retrograde, you may discover themes of growth, especially concerning education, travel, and philosophy. Some new ideas you have may be questioned, so you'll need to decide whether or not you should adopt a different point of view.

ADVICE: When the planet of growth is retrograde, we have an opportunity to test out some of our new theories! Take this time to practice new ideas about the world and society.

PLAN:

_____

_____

_____

Saturn

FREQUENCY: Once per year

LENGTH: About 140 days

IMPACT: Medium

MEANING: Saturn governs our rules and responsibilities. Unsurprisingly, Saturn retrograde does not allow us to cut corners. It lifts Saturn's limits and allows us to revisit what we've done during the rest of its orbit. If we tried to rush through a project or take a shortcut, Saturn retrograde will bring us back to show us where we've learned the wrong lessons.

ADVICE: Go back to key experiences to guarantee that they've been addressed correctly. If you've confronted your problems responsibly, Saturn will reward your hard work. If you've been living in denial however, Saturn will be sure to challenge this approach.

PLAN:

Uranus

FREQUENCY: Once per year

LENGTH: About 148 days

IMPACT: Low

MEANING: When Uranus is retrograde, surprises may not always be transparent. Uranus loves shock value. When it goes backward, its impact is often psychological. Uranus retrograde will have you reconsidering the way you think.

ADVICE: Uranus retrograde is a perfect time to release old, toxic patterns and adopt new, out-of-the-box thinking. This is a chance to try something different!

PLAN:

Neptune

FREQUENCY: Once per year

LENGTH: About 150 days

IMPACT: Low

MEANING: Neptune spends nearly 40 percent of its orbit retrograde. In many ways, Neptune's backward glide defines its spirit. Neptune represents fantasy and illusion, so during the planet's reverse phase, we are encouraged to backpedal through any fog we can't see through.

ADVICE: Neptune retrograde isn't about clarity. It's about sitting in the discomfort and embracing the unknown. Don't be afraid to get dreamy!

PLAN:

Pluto

FREQUENCY: Once per year

LENGTH: About 180 days

IMPACT: Low

MEANING: Pluto spends almost half of its orbit retrograde, and its retrograde is a big part of its purpose. When the planet glides in reverse, we reconsider how we are personally impacted by ideas of control.

ADVICE: Pluto retrograde is the time to release yourself from smothering relationships. Alternatively, if you are the one being controlling, Pluto retrograde will suggest that you loosen your grip.

PLAN:

Part Four

Your Universe

Putting It All Together

Congratulations, Cosmic Warrior!

You now have all the tools you need to launch into the stars and live a celestial life!

On the next page, you will put it all together. This last reflection is all about defining your unique universe. I leave you with these questions:

What defines your core? Write it in the sun.

What are the stars and planets of your life? What are the ideas, values, and people that are important to you? Show how they orbit you.

Where are your black holes, your challenges and obstacles? Place them in your universe.

Get creative! This is *your* galaxy! You are the center of your own world, so celebrate what it means to be YOU.

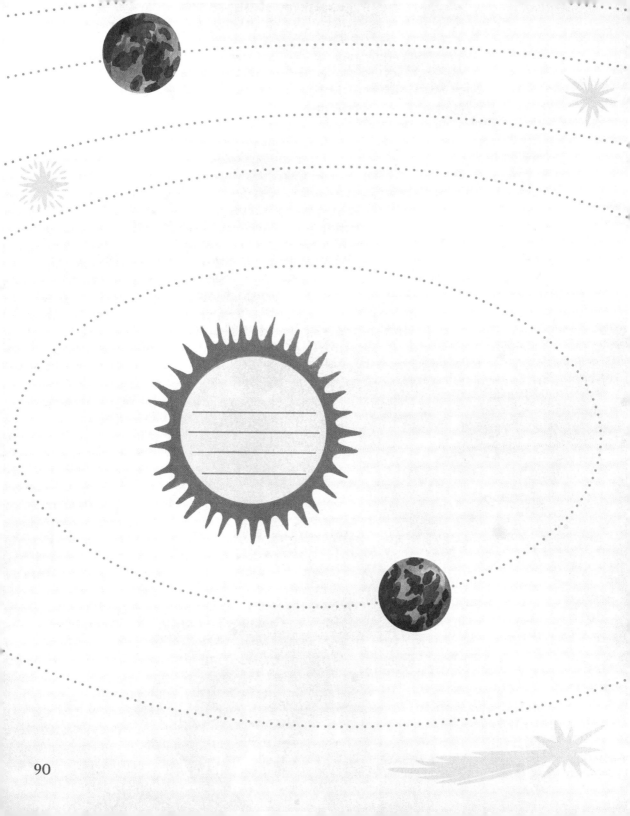

Index

About the Author

Aliza Kelly is a New York City-based astrologer, author, and host of Cosmopolitan's show Star Chart. Aliza's horoscopes and cosmic columns appear in *Cosmopolitan* and *Allure*, and her work has been featured in *BuzzFeed*, *Vogue*, *PAPER*, *Bustle*, *Refinery29*, *HuffPost*, and *Girlboss*. In her private practice, Aliza hosts monthly workshops and provides chart readings for her clientele. This is her first book for Cosmic Warriors of all ages.

Notes

Notes